# What Our Readers Have Said...

## Applicability

*"These books are great tools that should be used as guidelines for our everyday supervisory practices. You need to take the time to do a short self-evaluation when reading them."*

•

*"The Pinpoint Training Series delivers information that could be used in a lot different areas."*

•

*"The things and problems we deal with everyday are discussed in these books."*

## Convenience

*"I like this because I can take them with me to read at a convenient time. I feel the little time I have to spend in the office is best use on activities that directly relate to revenue opportunities. I like the short amount of time it takes to keep up with these."*

•

*"I prefer the self-study approach; it fits in with my schedule."*

•

*"I like the fact that the format allows the books to be reviewed as time permits. All work has been conducted on personal, evening/weekend time."*

•

*"Easy to use... if you put the time into it."*

**Challenge**

*"My thought is that the real value of these books comes into effect when doing the action plans."*

•

*"I like the fact that the format allows assignments to be reviewed as time permits."*

**Clarity**

*"Short and sweet. These books are easy to comprehend."*

•

*"Easy to use, understand, and reference if needed."*

**Relevance**

*"I have enjoyed reading these books. They are relevant to today's work environment and the ongoing change in the way we manage our workforce."*

•

*"I believe the contents of the Pinpoint series are excellent. It causes one to reflect on the daily dynamics in working with oneself as well as with management and peers."*

# Negative Workplace Behaviors

*Pinpoint Leadership Skill Development Training Series*

TIMOTHY F. BEDNARZ

MAJORIUM
BUSINESS PRESS

Pinpoint Leadership Skill Development Training Series
*"Negative Workplace Bahaviors"*
Timothy F. Bednarz

Graphic design: Monika Pawlak

Majorium Business Press
2025 Main Street
Stevens Point, WI 54481
715.342.1018 • 800.654.4935



ISBN 978-1-62101-048-7

Printed in the United States of America

# Introduction

*The Pinpoint Leadership Skill Development Training Series* is designed for targeted training and education regarding increased improvement in a specific skill or competency.

Each book within this series is designed to be easy to use, understand and apply to your job. It can be used as a basis for training individuals, as a discussion guide or as a personal training tool.

Each chapter within this book discusses a specific concept. When you have completed all eight chapters you should have a 360° perspective of the topic.

Additionally, each chapter is divided into specific sections:

- The first section provides you with an overview of the topic
- The Implications section discusses why the concept is important, and why it is important to learn and apply.
- The Strategies, Tips & Techniques to Apply section teaches how to use and apply the particular concept to your work.
- The Points to Ponder section gives you something to think about or to be discussed with a group setting. These are questions not meant to be immediately answered, but to be pondered over time.
- The Training Activity section provides you with the tools to transfer what you have learned to your job. It is designed to help create an action plan to effectively apply the concept.

Each of the topics in this series is time-tested and proven in the marketplace. They have been used by thousands of employees as training tools. Many of the users have commented that what made these books valuable, was the ability to refer to them when a problem surfaced. They indicated that they remembered reading about the exact problem. They referred back to these books and found an appropriate solution.

You will find them equally valuable as a resource in your professional development library.

# Table of Contents

## LEARNING OBJECTIVES:

- To interpret and analyze the critical factors and benefits of interaction within an organization.
- To overcome problems and pitfalls related to leader and employee interaction.
- To apply specific strategies to enhance workplace interaction.
- To understand and identify the negative consequences of failing to develop effective interaction principles, practices and evaluation.
- To analyze the expected results and outcomes of developing and sustaining workplace interaction.
- To apply effective strategies to develop and enhance workplace, organizational and leadership interaction and interactivity.

# 1

# Creating Positive Behavioral Standards Are Key to Developing a Non-Hostile Work Environment

The evolution from manager to leader is not an easy path to follow. While the principles and theories that apply to leadership are straightforward, their actual application in the real world is often another matter altogether. The courage and convictions of a leader are put to the test in the workplace environment, where one of the biggest trials is in dealing with negative employee behavior.

## IMPLICATIONS — WHAT THIS MEANS TO YOU

By definition, leadership requires one to actively work at eliminating negative workplace behaviors and actions. It is the leader's role to ensure that consistent behavioral standards, free from personal bias, are applied to all members under his or her direction. Inconsistent standards will often only create additional workplace problems that take up more of the leader's time and effort.

All organizations should have clearly defined consequences for inappropriate behavior, because what happens in the workplace can dramatically affect a company, its leaders and employees. In fact, behavioral ramifications can extend beyond the company itself, even into a courtroom. One only need examine the increase of employee lawsuits related to harassment and other inappropriate behaviors. Leaders are liable for their handling of related complaints, and, if not thorough and careful, they can inadvertently expose the company to both civil and criminal litigation.

Beyond protecting against liability issues, when leaders effectively manage workplace behaviors, they can positively and dramatically impact the overall performance of their unit. Allowing inappropriate and unwelcome behaviors to go uncorrected undermines the effectiveness of the unit. It is the leader's job to assure an atmosphere of mutual respect exists in the workplace if they wish to maximize efficiency and productivity.

## STRATEGIES, TIPS & TECHNIQUES TO APPLY

Leaders must create an atmosphere where specific standards of appropriate business and workplace behaviors are consistently applied and enforced. This requires the leader to eliminate employee behaviors and attitudes that interfere with the organizational unit's performance.

Leaders can posture themselves in two distinct ways. The first is to be firm in emphasizing that negative behaviors will not be tolerated. In this case, the leader might threaten legal and corporate action as a consequence for misbehavior. Although some leaders find this approach effective, many targeted subordinates are not motivated to change because they do not understand how their actions can warrant such severe penalties. As such, this approach gives them no incentive to alter or modify their personal behaviors.

A better approach is to develop and apply behavioral standards that emphasize their impact on the unit's effectiveness and productivity. Individuals like to work in a stress-free environment. And when behavioral standards are consistently applied and enforced, unwelcome, stressful behaviors are eliminated. Leaders thus create a more productive and respectful work environment.

Appropriate and consistent behavioral standards do not create a sterile and constricted atmosphere where every individual action, word and gesture must be watched. Instead, they create an environment where leaders and subordinates develop mutual trust, respect and rapport. This is the cornerstone for building productive workgroups that eventually evolve into self-directing teams.

When leaders fail to address and curtail personality conflicts, bullying, vulgarities, uninvited behaviors or undesirable comments, they surrender their capacity to lead. Truly effective leaders confront these issues proactively. They foresee the negative impact of bad behaviors, and harness conviction and courage to quickly remedy problems before they spread.

Oftentimes, corrective actions include making difficult decisions. Each leader must personally develop and apply codes and standards based on company policies and principles. The central focus is to eliminate offensive or threatening behaviors, attitudes and actions in a positive, productive way. Once negative behaviors are eliminated, the organizational unit's integrity and respect are restored.

Most leaders find it easier to prevent harmful workplace behaviors from developing in the first place than having to deal with them after the fact. Leaders can be proactive by fully educating employees about expected behavior and the consequences for not adhering to the standards set.

Additionally, leaders should actively monitor and observe individual behaviors, intervening when necessary. To further protect themselves from liability, leaders must maintain accurate and objective records of inappropriate employee actions.

## POINTS TO PONDER — SOMETHING TO THINK ABOUT

1. Is your business environment worker-friendly or hostile? Is it harmonious or disrupted by conflict?
2. Have you personally participated in or witnessed behaviors that were unwelcome, uninvited, unsolicited, undesirable or inappropriate?

## TRAINING ACTIVITY – APPLICATION & ACTION PLAN

Perform an evaluation of the workplace environment you supervise.

1. Identify specific behaviors that have interfered with individual performance.
2. Determine if these behaviors are detrimental.
3. Pinpoint additional behaviors you have observed that were unwelcome, uninvited, unsolicited, undesirable or inappropriate.
4. Determine the seriousness of these behaviors, and identify how they can be addressed and eliminated.

# 2

# The Impact of Hostile Actions and Behaviors in the Workplace

Hostile actions and behaviors in the workplace create a demeaning environment that has a definite negative impact upon worker performance and effectiveness. Inappropriate behaviors also jeopardize an organizational unit's morale and productivity as a whole.

## IMPLICATIONS — WHAT THIS MEANS TO YOU

The term "hostile workplace environment" takes into account both physical and emotional destructive workplace behaviors. It encompasses the specific conduct that negatively affects workers in a company and continues on in the absence of immediate and direct intervention. In other words, a hostile workplace environment exists when negative behaviors and actions are deemed "allowable."

Many leaders are often confused about what constitutes a hostile workplace environment and are unsure about the associated legal ramifications. Because the issues pertaining to such an environment are not always clear-cut, it leaves many leaders unclear about the measures necessary to combat any problems, issues and concerns.

## STRATEGIES, TIPS & TECHNIQUES TO APPLY

Many people do not agree about what actions and behaviors constitute "hostility." As such, leaders often struggle with ambiguous areas when determining guidelines for appropriate conduct in their workplace. Some actions may be immediately recognizable as "hostile" while others are deemed "unacceptable." Regardless of these distinctions, both types need to be dealt with before they lead to a crisis that can include potential legal issues. Leaders can prevent a crisis by taking the following actions:

### Provide Guidance about the Seriousness of the Issue

Leaders need to stress to their employees that appropriate behavior includes more than just motives: individuals are accountable for the negative consequences of all their workplace actions, even if the outcome is unintentional. The presence of negative outcomes in the workplace is key to defining a hostile environment.

Part of a leader's role is to commit themselves to fostering a workplace free of harassment and intimidation. A non-hostile environment allows all members to work together with openness, trust and respect for one another and their differences. A non-hostile climate lets employees perform their jobs and assignments without ridicule, intimidation or a lack of consideration. Intimidation and any form of harassment or inappropriateness undermine an organizational unit's morale, productivity and effectiveness.

Employees need to be made aware that any form of harassment or hostility on their part will officially be considered misconduct; all inappropriate behaviors will lead to disciplinary action. Penalties for continuous misconduct should be plainly stated, the most serious being termination of employment. To necessitate a change in behavior or prevent negative behavior in the first place, leaders need to clearly stress accountability and responsibility for one's own actions.

### Educate to Define and Prevent Offending Actions and Behaviors

It is up to the leader to educate employees about his or her expectations by defining offensive workplace actions and behaviors. All employees should be expected to exhibit high ethical standards of honesty and integrity based on the company's core values, code of professional ethics, principles, or other applicable policies.

Leaders must stress that everyone should always avoid behavior that may create an atmosphere of hostility or intimidation. All individuals, regardless of rank in the company, are expected to treat each other with courtesy and respect. Inappropriate behavior can include vandalizing property and making belittling comments, even if they are intended in a joking manner.

Workplace hostility often coincides with unwelcome verbal or physical behavior, whether a onetime or repeated event, that interferes with work or offends another person. Mildly offensive comments or behaviors can quickly become harassment when repeated, while a single incident is considered harassment if it is so severe that it immediately impacts the overall work environment or its employees.

## Recognize Specific Hostile Actions

There are ten basic types of behaviors and actions that play a large part in producing a hostile environment. Leaders must be constantly alert and intervene immediately when they notice these behaviors:

- Inappropriate and unwelcome comments, gestures or physical actions
- Severe or repeated insults to anyone in the workplace
- Direct or indirect racial slurs or negative stereotypes toward an individual or group
- Public or private temper tantrums
- Severe or repeated insults about another's personal or professional competence
- Threats or insults, whether vocal, written or sent electronically
- Deliberate destruction of workplace property, including informational materials, symbols, posters, equipment and books, etc.
- False or malicious complaints against other employees
- Repeated presence of individuals in groups that are singled out for negative attention

- Situations that cause personal embarrassment or humiliation, or that have demeaning or belittling consequences

## POINTS TO PONDER — SOMETHING TO THINK ABOUT

1. Have you educated your employees about what constitutes "workplace hostility"? Have you addressed both the legal and ethical ramifications of specific actions and behaviors?
2. In your leadership role, are you always on the watch for negative behaviors and actions? Do you provide immediate intervention when you see them? Or do you wait for reports to come to you before observing and acting?

## TRAINING ACTIVITY — APPLICATION & ACTION PLAN

Over the next week, observe to see if any hostile behaviors are occurring within your area of supervision.

1. Keep a list of the negative behaviors and actions that occur frequently.
2. Prepare a presentation to discuss the ethical, work-related and legal issues of such actions and behaviors.
3. Address the consequences of allowing these inappropriate behaviors to continue.
4. Take time to set up a meeting with all your employees to educate them about these issues.

# 3

# Workplace Aggression and Violence... Are Your Organizational Unit Members at Risk?

According to most reports, the frequency and severity of workplace aggression and violence are increasing. Workplace violence is defined as the intent to cause harm to one or more individuals or an organization through either direct or indirect actions. Although many forms of indirect violence and aggression may not produce actual physical damage, some will nevertheless be destructive and harmful.

## IMPLICATIONS — WHAT THIS MEANS TO YOU

Passive-aggressive behavior has a definite impact upon the workplace in a number of ways. Leaders are often responsible for dealing with the workplace behavior of individuals whose actions may not be considered overtly aggressive but have the potential to trigger such a reaction in someone else: an aggressive action often leads to retaliation.

Leaders need to be aware of employees who display passive-aggressive behavior. This is the most common form of aggression in the workplace. This type of behavior can have tremendously negative consequences for all organizational unit members and the company as a whole, as it impacts workplace security, productivity, employee effectiveness and job satisfaction.

In order to prevent the organization and its employees from experiencing dire consequences, leaders must understand the reasons behind passive-aggressive behavior and the warning signs that often precede it.

## STRATEGIES, TIPS & TECHNIQUES TO APPLY

In most cases, aggressive or violent employees believe that their behavior is justified. It is up to leaders to assess the causes and reasons behind aggressive actions and behaviors. Doing so helps them identify high-risk warning signs and prevent violent behaviors from occurring in the first place. Discussed below are ways to proactively combat workplace aggression.

### Identify Causes for Violence and Aggression

When leaders look for the causes of workplace aggression or violence, the natural tendency is to only focus on the perpetrator initially. However, this response neglects to account for other employees who may be behind-the-scenes instigators. There are several such contributing factors that leaders must look for.

Dominance can be an important factor to consider when assessing possible aggression in the workplace. Research has shown that Type A personalities can be aggressive because of their dominant characteristics. These individuals usually work under significant stress, are easily frustrated and therefore have a high risk of aggression or violence.

Self-monitoring is another personality variable that affects aggressive behavior and violence. Self-monitoring refers to the way in which individuals are aware of how their behavior positively or negatively affects other employees. Individuals that lack self-monitoring are often oblivious to the impacts of their behavior. For the employees involved, a chain of hostility can be produced by the cause-and-effect relationship of their actions and reactions.

Social climate may directly contribute to hostility and aggression. A 1998 study on workplace violence and aggression by J.H. Neumann and R.A. Baron concluded that workplace social situations sometimes involve group-imposed norms (hidden from management) that permit or even promote various types of aggression and hostility. Furthermore, a disregard for certain social norms or guidelines by members of the group may cause resentment or hostility that lead to retaliatory violence.

## Identify Warning Signs of High-Risk Individuals

In addition to examining some of the potential causes for workplace violence and aggression, it is helpful for leaders to analyze some of the warning signs that suggest an employee is at high risk for passive-aggression or violence. The following are several key behaviors to watch for:

*Notable changes* – When employees change their dress, attitudes or behaviors, or any other aspect of their daily work routine, it may indicate that something is amiss. Even though some changes may be good, unexplained behavior should be monitored over time.

*Deep depression* – When people are seriously depressed, they often do not care about themselves or what happens to them. They can display behaviors that are not typical. Although depressed individuals are rarely violent, it is a situation worth monitoring.

*Romantic obsession that is ignored or rejected* – Watching the news media nowadays, one realizes that office romances are becoming an increasing problem in many workplaces. Any problems should be monitored closely and weighed against company policies and rules.

*Continually blaming others* – If employees continually blame others for being nonproductive, less motivated or whatever else, it generally indicates they are frustrated or unhappy. These individuals might be inclined to act violently on their feelings.

*Highly frustrated* – Leaders should always monitor whether their employees experience increased work-related or personal frustration. Frustration often leads to direct or indirect aggression.

*Inability to accept criticism* – Most individuals do not like to be criticized, but employees that respond in an unusual, disproportionate or unreasonable way, need to be carefully monitored.

*Feelings of injustice or unfairness* – While these feelings are generally not abnormal or problematic, they are often an indication that a personnel problem may be emerging that should be evaluated. It is well worth the leader's time to explore the issue even though these feelings may not indicate violent or aggressive retaliatory action.

*Repeated disputes with others* – Employees who are always in conflict with coworkers are much more likely to behave aggressively or become hostile.

*A controlling or demanding presence* – Those who act in a controlling way or with a demanding presence, display existing aggression that might already be dangerous. However, it could also indicate problems that have the potential to create conflict with other employees.

## POINTS TO PONDER — SOMETHING TO THINK ABOUT

1. How often do you deal with passive-aggressive behaviors or actions in your organizational unit that could easily erupt into acts of overt aggression or violence?
2. Have you considered that an employee social group is operating behind the scenes with norms or guidelines that may encourage aggressive actions, hostility or possible violence?

## TRAINING ACTIVITY — APPLICATION & ACTION PLAN

1. Print out and keep the warning signs listed in this lesson for easy reference when assessing workplace aggression or violent situations.
2. List and monitor any observable aggressive behaviors or actions that are repeated over a period of time.
3. Attempt to determine the causes for the aggressive behaviors or actions, and identify the problems they caused.
4. Create a plan to prevent future occurrences and pinpoint possible high-risk individuals.

# 4

# Managing, Controlling and Preventing Workplace Hostility, Violence and Aggression

In today's workplace, violence can occur anytime and anywhere. Workplace violence is basically defined as: an act of physical aggression, threat of physical hurt, harassment, intimidation or any other disruptive behavior that occurs within a company. It can affect and involve managers, employees and even customers, contractors or visitors.

## IMPLICATIONS — WHAT THIS MEANS TO YOU

Leaders must be aware of the different actions and behaviors in the work environment that can trigger workplace violence. Causes may include a wide range of situations unrelated to work, such as domestic problems, a seriously ill child or other types of stress-creating issues.

Effective leaders understand the best prevention comes with identifying problems early and dealing with them immediately and effectively. The leader is responsible for communicating their expectations for workplace behavior up front. They need to stress individual accountability and responsibility and explain how each person's actions and behaviors contribute to a "good place to work."

Leaders also understand there are consequences for allowing aggressive and violent actions to continue. Certain actions, if they continue or go uncontrolled, may cause their company to be held liable for legal violations. Liability occurs if there is a recognized potential for workplace violence, and management fails to do anything to prevent or abate it.

## STRATEGIES, TIPS & TECHNIQUES TO APPLY

Leaders must take a primary role in the reduction of potential threats of aggression and violence. When they educate employees about behavioral expectations, they must establish parameters with specific guidelines for prevention and reporting. To reduce the threat of violence and prevent company liability, leaders must consistently maintain and address these guidelines.

### Guidelines to Reduce Violence and Aggression

- Trust "gut instincts." If leaders suspect something is occurring out of the norm, or feel something is not quite right, they are probably correct and need to act on it.
- Make the workplace as comfortable as it can be to reduce stress and personal negative incidents from occurring. Prevention is far better than dealing with the consequences.
- Create a partnership with employees. Highlight issues of potential violence and aggressive actions where all can work together for the benefit of one another and the organization. This develops an atmosphere of caring, respect and mutual trust.
- Recognize the factors related to domestic violence. Determine if any employees are potentially violent at home. Employees that are prone to domestic violence are likely to be aggressive in the workplace.
- Develop a plan for dealing with high-risk employees. Outline specific steps to take if a violent, hostile or aggressive situation emerges. Identify the appropriate person in human resources to contact and the immediate actions to take to handle the situation.
- Develop consistent and realistic procedures for grievances. If a grievance is dealt with reasonably, immediately and effectively, the situa-

tion is likely to remain under control. These procedures help reduce serious consequences and possible liability.

- It is a leader's responsibility to safeguard their employees and the workplace from former, possibly disgruntled, employees.
- Make it a point to safeguard vulnerable individuals. If a leader determines that certain individuals are at higher risk of becoming another's target of aggression or inappropriate behavior, protective steps should be taken.

One of the major causes of workplace violence and aggression is in organizations that maintain "politicized" environments where frustration and mistrust exist between management and employees. This type of organizational climate produces negative feelings that may actively breed direct or indirect aggression. Effective leaders combat politicization by creating an open environment that eliminates barriers.

There are six key procedures for reducing potential violence and aggression in the workplace:

- Leaders need to create an open communication environment where employees can freely discuss problems and concerns that affect them.
- Leaders must listen carefully to become fully aware of concerns, issues, potential problems, dissatisfied employees and high-risk situations. Aggression and violence are best prevented when leaders pay attention and actively listen to what is going on in their workplace. They must discuss employee concerns and show they care. Active listening and appropriate responses may help identify and clarify problems before they become explosive or destructive.
- Leaders need to relieve their employees' unnecessary stress. Keeping individuals well informed can help minimize stress by eliminating unnecessary fear and anxiety. Effective leaders make it a point to answer questions directly and honestly, to the best of their ability. They actively search for existing and emerging problems or concerns that, once discovered, are appropriately addressed to reduce fear and anxiety. With all these efforts combined, leaders help create a comfortable medium for addressing issues, solving problems and finding answers.

- Leaders need to educate their employees on all the issues surrounding workplace violence and aggression. Communication and trust are top priorities with this procedure. An informed and educated workforce is easier to manage and generally has fewer problems.
- Effective leaders make sure their employees are trained in conflict management and negotiation. This procedure helps minimize potential eruptions of aggressive or violent behavior. It also reinforces employee accountability and responsibility. They attempt to settle a dispute before it gets to the point where the leader has to step in to do damage control.
- Leaders need to be good role models and lead by example. This means effectively communicating and demonstrating how to manage stress, listen, and deal with controversy and conflict in ways that produce positive results for everyone. Employees learn through observation. It is extremely important that they consistently see their leaders behaving rationally, considerately and ethically.

## POINTS TO PONDER — SOMETHING TO THINK ABOUT

1. Do you believe your work environment contains elements of frustration, mistrust and obvious or hidden aggression?
2. Have you established guidelines that lay out preventive measures for addressing workplace aggression, hostility or violence? Have you used or developed intervention procedures? If so, do they work as you expected them to?

## TRAINING ACTIVITY – APPLICATION & ACTION PLAN

Analyze your current program to see how your established responses to workplace violence, aggression or hostility compare with the ones discussed in this lesson. Your program should include the following:

1. Take preventative steps that actively look for and deal with specific causes of violence and aggression
2. Each act should be targeted as a unique occurrence: all types of violence and aggression cannot be handled in the same manner.
3. A combination of intervention actions is necessary to effectively deal with complex hostility and aggression.
4. Responses to potentially dangerous situations must be dealt with immediately.
5. Intervention or prevention programs must be developed and improved upon with the involvement and participation of all employees.
6. Have a long-term philosophy: problems not dealt with today become more problems for tomorrow.

# 5

# Sexual Harassment: Factors, Impact and Intervention

Sexual harassment impacts an organization's success because it jeopardizes employees' feelings of security. This in turn leads to decreased job satisfaction with increased turnover and absenteeism rates. As morale goes down, employees become less productive and may make ineffective decisions while exhibiting a decrease in motivation, performance and effectiveness.

## IMPLICATIONS – WHAT THIS MEANS TO YOU

Leaders must take an active role in addressing workplace sexual harassment. This includes understanding the factors behind it and taking effective steps for addressing a problem if and when it surfaces. The leader's main responsibility in this area is to help educate employees in how to take personal responsibility for their actions and decrease the likelihood of harassment occurring.

Leaders need to understand not only the serious effects of harassment on the performance of their organizational unit and employees but also the company's legal liability—with most of the responsibility falling to managers and leaders—when dealing with these issues. By effectively preparing the workplace for harassment issues, a leader engages in good business practices and keeps his or her company in compliance with the law.

## STRATEGIES, TIPS & TECHNIQUES TO APPLY

Employees must understand the many factors involved in sexual harassment in order to protect themselves and cope effectively with these sensitive issues. Leaders can help their employees by going over the specific factors that constitute sexual harassment and the decision making strategies that are in place for dealing with any potential issues that may arise.

### Factors That Warrant Sexual Harassment Complaints

Sexual harassment is defined as: Any unwelcome sexual advance, request for sexual favors of any kind, either verbally or nonverbally, or physical conduct of a sexual nature that unreasonably interferes with work, alters or is made a condition of employment, or creates an intimidating, hostile or offensive workplace environment. It is one form of sexual discrimination and, as such, is subject to the full extent of discrimination law.

The Equal Employment Opportunity Commission (EEOC) has established six guidelines for identifying sex and gender discrimination. Leaders must evaluate these guidelines if a complaint is filed. They are summarized as follows:

- Harassers may be men and women, and targets can be of either sex.
- A harasser doesn't necessarily have to be a supervisor or manager. It can be a coworker, a non-employee, an employer agent or a supervisor from another area within the parent company—even from a different geographic location.
- Same-sex harassment is given careful consideration. If leaders suspect this is occurring, they should determine whether or not the harasser treats members of one sex differently than the other.
- Victims do not have to be the direct targets of harassment. It is possible, for instance, that the sexual harassment of one female creates a hostile work environment for other females in the workplace who were not directly subjected to the harasser's attacks.
- Sexual harassment is not determined based on tangible economic injury as a direct result of the harasser's conduct. In other words, sexual

advances constitute harassment when they interfere with the victim's job or create a hostile work environment, whether or not a demotion or lost promotion of the harassed person is the result.

- An official sexual harassment reporting policy must be implemented; otherwise, legal liability may become an issue if a claim is filed. A company may also face liability if channels to report issues of harassment are not formally established.

When complaints are made to managers, leaders and others who are responsible for handling sexual harassment issues, the EEOC law does not require the company to immediately report the concern to authorities. However, all reports must be investigated immediately and thoroughly. Liability for the company arises from inadequately following established procedures once a complaint has been made.

## Conduct That Does and Does Not Constitute Sexual Harassment

Employees must have reasonable grounds before making any complaints of sexual harassment. Leaders must keep in mind that not all situations appearing to meet the definition of sexual harassment are ultimately determined to be instances of harassment. There is a wide range of ambiguous behavior that might offend some individuals but not others.

The way to decide which actions qualify as sexual harassment is to determine whether or not the action was unwelcome. One key indicator of uninvited behavior is when the recipient—if the opportunity is safely available to him or her—asks the alleged harasser to stop the behavior.

There are some instances when individuals make remarks or gestures unaware of the effect their words and actions have on others. These individuals may simply be trying to flatter someone, when, unbeknown to them, they are actually causing great pain.

While sexual harassment typically involves demonstrating a pattern of behavior, it can occur in one single incident.

Leaders must keep their eyes open to observe actions and behaviors that are considered to be legitimate grounds for sexual harassment claims. Immediate and corrective action is required if any of the conditions listed below appear to be occurring within the workplace:

- An individual makes repetitive suggestive comments.
- Someone displays materials of a sexual nature, such as pornographic websites or screen savers, as well as pictures, posters, statues, etc.
- Crude or obscene language or gestures are used, including the telling of risqué or offensive jokes.
- Someone makes repeated and/or exaggerated compliments about another employee's personal appearance.
- Persistent invitations to social activities are made even though the recipient conveyed that it was unwelcome.
- Deliberate and physical contact of an unsolicited nature occurs.
- Two employees display persistent close physical proximity where one individual has expressed his or her discomfort with the situation.

Before considering bringing about a complaint, employees need to do the following:

- Review their sexual harassment work policy, rules and regulations.
- Keep a log of the details of the offensive behavior: a journal with dates and times is valid supportive evidence.
- Follow the guidelines of the employer's sexual harassment policy.
- Employees should then use the following decision making strategies:
- Decide whether the conduct was unwelcome, unsolicited or offensive.
- Determine whether the conduct was repeated, noting if the recipient told the offender that the behavior was unwelcome or offensive.
- Did the behavior involve a supervisor-employee relationship where one person had power and authority over the other?
- Did the conduct have substantially severe results because of verbal, physical, hostile, disruptive, continuous, persuasive, or provoking actions or behavior?
- Determine whether individuals exhibiting sexual behavior were given any sort of preferential treatment that ultimately had a negative effect on others in the workplace.

- Decide if a hypothetical "reasonable person" would be negatively affected in a similar circumstance.

### POINTS TO PONDER – SOMETHING TO THINK ABOUT

1. Have you made it a practice to understand the factors involved in sexual harassment issues in order to discuss it with your employees?
2. Have you educated your employees on how to apply the proper decision making strategies when it comes to sexual harassment issues and complaints?

### TRAINING ACTIVITY – APPLICATION & ACTION PLAN

1. Conduct a brainstorming session in which employees generate a list of behaviors and offenses that would be considered legitimate reasons for filing a sexual harassment claim.
2. Create a list of criteria that employees can use to individually evaluate a complaint. Use the criteria outlined in this lesson, and add others that are suggested.
3. Solidify the steps that seem reasonable to follow for reporting a sexual harassment claim.

# 6

# Inappropriate Behaviors Create Workplace Conflict

There are certain inappropriate behaviors that may not be particularly prone to produce hostility or retaliation, but can be warning signs of a coming escalation. If left unchecked, these behaviors can intensify into workplace conflict and eventually lead to a full-scale hostile work environment.

Inappropriate behaviors are appearing more frequently in the workplace. SACS Consulting and Investigative Services, a company specializing in workplace conflict solutions, conducted an investigation into inappropriate behaviors that had a negative effect on employees. They found that over several years, workplaces witnessed a tenfold increase in personal altercations stemming from issues that caused high levels of conflict and stress in organizational units.

## IMPLICATIONS — WHAT THIS MEANS TO YOU

Recently, the U.S. Department of Labor estimated that over 500,000 employees currently lose close to 1.2 million workdays because of physical and mental stress and other health concerns that are related to inappropriate workplace behavior.

Leaders need to be aware of several inappropriate behaviors that increase conflict and then identify the factors behind them to understand how to deal with the offending employees. Individuals generally do not report these types of inappropriate behaviors as often as they would others because they view them as more annoying than hostile. Additionally, people who are subjected to such behavior often fear they will be picked on even more in retaliation for their complaints.

If these inappropriate behaviors are left unchecked, leaders will notice a decline in motivation and productivity as well as attitude changes in organizational unit members. This situation leaves the door open for hostility and overt aggression that can fuel a more violent workplace atmosphere.

## STRATEGIES, TIPS & TECHNIQUES TO APPLY

Leaders must address three specific behaviors that cause undue conflict within their organizational unit: inappropriate horseplay, name-calling and the invasion of personal space. These actions can be grouped together because all three are intimidating behaviors that can produce high levels of workplace conflict and stress.

A fourth inappropriate behavior, email abuse, is addressed as a separate issue because of its serious consequences. Email abuse can also instigate high levels of conflict in the workplace, but, more importantly, it has the ability to create severe legal liability for a company.

### Inappropriate Horseplay

Inappropriate horseplay generally includes outright teasing, belittling, pushing, shoving, tripping, tickling and emotional mind games. It can have a negative effect on many em ployees. Employees who use this type of behavior project their inadequacies and shortcomings to gain the recognition of others. Most individuals who resort to inappropriate horseplay generally do not realize that it can be considered harassment.

### Name-Calling

Name-calling is an act of vocally intimidating others with inappropriate stereotypes and undesirable phrases or words. Employees who resort to name-calling generally have the tendency to challenge authority and others. They resort to tactless comments, often in an aggressive way.

Name-calling produces instant conflict that can lead to retaliation. This behavior can easily create a hostile, unfriendly workplace environment.

## Invasion of Personal Space

The unwelcome invasion of one's personal space may be abusive and intimidating. It includes unwarranted interruptions, standing too close during conversations, undesirable touching and other behaviors that disrupt an individual's focus or threaten one's personal comfort level.

This behavior can be considered harassment even though it is not actively hostile. It is a violation if the behavior is unwelcome and/or intrudes upon someone else's feeling of security. Invasion of personal space greatly impacts others because it disturbs their feelings of comfort, well-being and stability.

Such inappropriate behavior decreases worker motivation and effectiveness and produces conflict that diminishes productivity. Employees engaged in this type of behavior are often self-centered and have little consideration for how their actions affect others.

All three general behaviors discussed above are potentially destructive and should be eliminated before they have a direct negative impact on employees. Leaders can effectively address inappropriate horseplay, name-calling and invasion of personal space with the following techniques:

- By posting guidelines, rules and consequences, leaders emphasize that these behaviors are to be taken seriously because of their potential impact on everyone.
- Leaders need to clearly define the expectations and rules governing these three types of behaviors. They should stress that each related action is potentially hurtful because it may cause intimidation and eventually lower the victim's self-esteem. Because inappropriate behavior often causes employees to lose focus on their jobs, leaders must firmly establish that an employee's repeated application of any damaging behaviors makes him or her personally responsible for decreasing overall productivity.
- Leaders should determine and apply specific consequences for inappropriate behavior, with the intention of eliminating or reducing their occurrence. Consequences can be designed to escalate with an increase in the frequency or number of offenses.

- Offending employees must be monitored to ensure that they eliminate their negative behavior. Monitoring strategies must be consistent and fair, where the employee is given frequent, positive feedback, if warranted. Treated in this manner, the employee's desire to change will increase, and he or she will become more accountable and responsible for their actions.
- Employees should be allowed to offer their input regarding how to handle inappropriate behaviors and subsequent corrective actions. Leaders can get their people involved by brainstorming guidelines and solutions to eliminate conflict. This process also helps employees personally be prepared to deal with an inappropriate behavior before it reaches confrontational levels. Brainstormed guidelines should become a standard for all to follow.
- Leaders will find it effective to ask their employees for input about what constitutes good reporting strategies and procedures. Employees are more comfortable reporting incidents when they have a say in developing methods that are less threatening to them.
- Leaders always maintain the responsibility to take effective actions to prevent inappropriate behaviors.

## Inappropriate Use and Abuse of Email

Abusive emails have become prominent. Employees carry on extended email conversations throughout the day. This medium makes it easy for individuals to pass along jokes or any number of other distractions. With online access privileges that can be easily misused, employees face temptations that can end with serious consequences.

Effective leaders understand their company may face great risks that come along with email abuse. Companies can be held liable for offensive communications made by employees using the business's Internet or email access. For example, in 1995, Chevron paid more than $2 million to settle a sexual harassment suit brought against it for offensive messages circulated via the corporate email system.

There are several ways to address email abuse in the workplace:

- Leaders must develop guidelines for appropriate and inappropriate email use. Email monitoring by the employer is a right of ownership. Employees also need to be made aware that when they are working they are on company time, and inappropriate or personal use of email constitutes the stealing of company time and resources.

- Leaders need to address both the legal issues associated with email and the productivity problems stemming from its abuse. Severe problems are brought about by "email overload," where the forwarding and CC features of email messages contribute to an overuse or abuse. Additionally, when employees distribute emails and have conversations on various topics, barrages of personal messages begin to bury more important company-related items. Some messages may require immediate attention but, as a result of being buried, are not addressed in a timely fashion. As a result, the company experiences a decrease in its overall efficiency and productivity.

## POINTS TO PONDER — SOMETHING TO THINK ABOUT

1. Does your unit experience employees that resort to any of the inappropriate behaviors discussed in this lesson? Have you detailed guidelines and consequences for their actions?
2. Does your company have an email policy? Have you addressed the legal issues of inappropriate email and the time and productivity issues involved?

## TRAINING ACTIVITY — APPLICATION & ACTION PLAN

As an organizational unit, brainstorm effective guidelines to help eliminate conflict and come up with ways to cope with inappropriate behaviors before they become confrontational.

- Discuss why the inappropriate behaviors mentioned in this lesson are abusive, offensive and intimidating.
- Develop reporting procedures and strategies that employees are comfortable with.
- Come up with a list of consequences the unit feels are fair and just.
- Use these guidelines as a standard for all to follow.

# 7

# When There Is Conflict... There Is usually a "Bully" at Work

When workplace conflicts surface, it is often the result of a "bully." In a normal work environment, 1 out of every 30 people is an active bully. Bullying is the most common cause of harassment, discrimination, prejudice, abuse, conflict and violence in the workplace.

## IMPLICATIONS – WHAT THIS MEANS TO YOU

There is a tendency to overlook the negative impact a bully has on other employees. Unfortunately, the consequences of bullying can permeate the entire organization like a cancer. Bullies continually instigate conflict and lower productivity, creating fear, intimidation and turmoil behind the scenes. Often the immediate causes of conflict are hidden because bullies are masters of deception. If the aforementioned estimate is correct, then most leaders have bullies in their workplace who are innocent and charming in the open and yet secretly vindictive.

It is important for leaders to understand that all bullies primarily want power, control and domination over others in order to mask their incompetence and inadequacies. The only thing that varies among bullies is the way they pursue their objectives. A major problem leaders face in remedying a bully issue is that bullies often commit offenses that are within the law rather than overtly aggressive actions that can be dealt with officially.

Leaders must grasp how bullies exert power and intimidation over others so easily. With knowledge of their inherent characteristics, leaders can figure out how to deal with bullies effectively. If a bully's actions are not curtailed, leaders will see a string of employees quit with little or no explanation, take more than normal personal health leaves, or work with minimal enthusiasm.

## STRATEGIES, TIPS & TECHNIQUES TO APPLY

### Why Bullies Are Able to Dominate Other Employees

Bullies are masters of self-interest and self-preservation. They find it necessary to intimidate and dominate others because their worst fear is to be exposed for their own inadequacies and incompetence.

Most cases of workplace bullying, regardless of the size of the company, involve only one or two instigators. The reason that so few are active is that bullies compete with one another, and the weaker individuals eventually give way to the more powerful. Understanding the factors surrounding bullying behaviors include:

- Employees may actually become dependent on a bully's behavior. The bully often has the power to get them through the day without making their work life difficult. Bullies thus establish the rules and atmosphere of obedience.
- Bullies often convince another employee to support them. This other employee essentially becomes their spokesperson or advocate.
- Many employees for one reason or another are easily taken in by the bully's charm, nature and deception. Sensing their ability to maintain power over others and the subsequent respect they receive, bullies feel enabled to continue their behavior. They are seen as mature on the outside despite immaturity lurking below the surface.
- Employees find it difficult to report bullying because they fear the

bully's retaliation or a lack of belief from their associates. Many employees will find it hard to gain the support of their coworkers against a bully because only the bully's targets are privy to his or her dual personality. The rest of the workplace only sees his or her charming side.

## Identifying a Bully's Characteristics

Leaders must be able to interpret several characteristics that identify bullies in their organizational unit. Once identified, it becomes easier to closely observe the methods they employ to intimidate and control other employees. Some characteristics to watch for include:

- Active bullies are generally more incompetent on the job. They use intimidating behaviors to hide this incompetence.
- Bullies prefer rule-based or procedurally-orientated jobs. These types of jobs require no imagination. Bullying behavior is often revealed when bullies are put into jobs or situations that compel them to deal with other employees.
- Bullies generally avoid accepting responsibility—even for their own behavior. When confronted, bullies instinctively deny everything. They also tend to trivialize everything in an attempt to divert a conversation. Bullies will do anything to keep their true nature a secret. If they do not, it may force them to do what they really don't want to do—face or acknowledge the harm their actions cause for others.
- Bullies continually counterattack and use counter-criticism techniques. They distort facts, fabricating them if necessary. These techniques are used to avoid answering any questions that may compel them to accept responsibility for their behavior or actions or to sidestep responses that may disclose their inadequacies.
- Bullies like to take the stance of a victim, often proclaiming that they are the sufferers of persecution. They are clever at manipulating others through their emotions, especially by utilizing guilt. Bullies easily display emotional outbursts—crying, self-pity, pretending to be devastated, even outwardly and loudly proclaiming *they* are being bullied.

## Dealing with Bullying Behavior Effectively

- When dealing with bullies, there is one rule, and one rule only: Never appease them. Discussing the situation never stops their behavior from recurring. While on the surface they appear to be conciliatory, behind the scenes the bullying continues unabated.
- Use direct eye contact when addressing a bully. Be careful not to succumb to their deviousness or extremely polite facade. Direct eye contact gives the leader control instead of the bully guiding and manipulating the direction of the conversation.
- Establish severe consequences for their behavior. It is only effective if the consequences leave the bully feeling there is no choice but to immediately alter his or her conduct.
- Request that all employees report any mistreatment from anybody bullying them in the workplace. Establish a comfortable method of reporting, and be consistent with the consequences. Doing this quickly sends a message to all employees, especially to the bullies, that there is a high price to pay for inappropriate actions.
- Sometimes it is feasible to transfer a bully to a job that is more isolated, but where he or she can still perform adequately. This solution, however, is often what a bully desires, and their behavior is a means to that end.
- Suggest to the bully they need to seek professional help. This may be required as a condition of employment if his or her behavior warrants it.
- There must be zero-tolerance for this kind of behavior in the workplace. Bullying is completely self-destructive and extremely hostile and intimidating.
- Keep an accurate record of a bully's behavior and any related reports made by other employees. This documentation is essential to terminate a bully if the need arises as well as protect employers from possible legal violations associated with the bullying that may result in fines or penalties.

## POINTS TO PONDER — SOMETHING TO THINK ABOUT

1. Have you had reports of any incidents or conflicts that resulted from a bully operating in your organizational unit? How did you approach the issue?
2. Do employees generally feel uneasy reporting a bully in the workplace? If so, do you think your established reporting procedures and consequences for bullying may be part of the reason?

## TRAINING ACTIVITY — APPLICATION & ACTION PLAN

1. As an organizational unit, list the characteristics of a bully.
2. Define what constitutes bullying as well as what does not.
3. Detail and define specific consequences for bullying, making sure the consequences are appropriate for the severity of the behavior.
4. Discuss why it is important to report bullying behavior.
5. Develop reporting procedures that employees feel comfortable with.

# 8

# Strategies and Techniques for Handling Workplace Complaints, Concerns and Issues

Leaders in the workplace hear several complaints every day. Some are minor and easily resolved; others are more complex, requiring complicated solutions. Leaders should have a specific procedure or decision tree set up to guide them through the resolution process fairly and consistently.

Decision trees come in different varieties, some more suited to particular issues than others. One type can be quite logical, providing the leader with a rather intuitive model to follow for simple problems. Difficult problems, on the other hand, require more complex models that give leaders the more intricate guidance they require.

## IMPLICATIONS – WHAT THIS MEANS TO YOU

Unresolved complaints are symptomatic of underlying issues in the workplace. When left unsettled, these issues fester and ultimately surface as major problems that can impact productivity, efficiency and performance, as well as expose an organization to legal liabilities. Leaders must always strive to resolve a problem; otherwise, employees who continually complain about the same issue yet don't see action being taken likely have legal recourse. Even a seemingly minor issue can have potential legal ramifications that make the company liable for failing to address the complaint.

Effective leaders understand the importance of immediately addressing and resolving complaints. They know that lingering issues hinder the performance of their organizational unit by disrupting the harmony and balance required to maximize output. Additionally, the time invested in "nipping a problem in the bud" is well spent when compared with the time required to deal with a complaint that has exploded into a major problem. Good leaders furthermore understand that a quick and effective response to a complaint limits the company's legal liability.

## STRATEGIES, TIPS & TECHNIQUES TO APPLY

Undoubtedly, leaders are well-versed in dealing with daily operational problems (e.g. production, quality, scheduling and efficiency) associated with the organizational unit's performance. And while it is possible these methods are effective at resolving related employee complaints, they are not the focus of this lesson. For present purposes, complaints will be limited to general workplace issues such as intimidation, harassment, bullying and other employee-related concerns.

When a complaint is initially brought to the leader's attention, he or she will most likely immediately classify it as a problem that is either major or minor. This tendency is natural, as quick classification leaves the leader with the necessary time and energy to identify and resolve the problem.

However, leaders must take care not to minimize a complaint. They need to recognize that it takes courage for an employee to voice a concern. In fact, before the complaint is made, quite often the issue has been going on for a sustained period, with the employee making many failed attempts at resolving it. Hence, it is important that the leader carefully consider the complaint's seriousness. Even if the individual tends to complain or whine about everything, each grievance should be examined on its own merits. If, after thoughtful consideration, the leader finds there isn't much to the complaint, then it may be dismissed. But a repeat pattern of similar complaints may require further action on the part of the leader. On the other hand, some employees rarely complain, and when they do the problem may be more serious than it initially appears.

Once the legitimacy of a complaint has been established, several steps must be taken. A decision tree, as outlined below, guides the leader to the ultimate solution.

## Preliminary Investigation

A preliminary investigation identifies underlying causes, the individuals involved and impacted, and the extent of the problem. When the problems causing the complaint are rooted out early, potential solutions can also be identified right away. If this is the case, leaders can act quickly to resolve the problem and move on to more pressing issues. If not, leaders must move on to the next step.

## Documentation

If the problem is bigger or more advanced than originally thought, then leaders must begin to document its extent—that is, the activities of the individuals causing the problem, and the complaints and actions of the employees affected by the problem.

Effective leaders understand the importance of documenting the problem: the process helps develop objective facts necessary for a satisfactory resolution and protects the company if the termination of employees is required.

## Interview All Participants

An initial investigation of a complaint and a documentation of the facts should include personal interviews with everyone involved in the issue. This gives all parties ample opportunity to express their viewpoints. Leaders must take care to stick with the facts and not be biased by previous experiences with anybody or let their personal feelings impact their decisions.

## Pinpoint the Causes and Solution

After interviewing all participants and listening carefully to what they had to say, leaders should be able to pinpoint the underlying causes of the problem. Sometimes the issue to be dealt with is obvious; in which case, immediate action is advised.

In more serious cases, leaders may need to consult with their superiors or the human resources professionals in their company to determine further action or attain recommendations. When issues of legal liability are involved in the solution, leaders must seek counsel from others more familiar with the issues. Effective leaders understand the limits of their responsibilities and the importance of calling on others with more expertise. When in doubt, it is best to call human resources to get their view on possible courses of action.

### Implement the Solution

Depending upon the seriousness of the problem and who is involved in crafting and implementing the solution, leaders must take action as soon as possible. Clearly, the solution can take many forms and have a variety of actions. As a result, leaders will often have to sit down with the people affected, either individually or together as a group.

In these sessions the problem will be plainly laid out, the findings and extent of the problem will be reported, and a discussion of the possible solutions initiated. In certain cases where the problem is very serious, solutions can be presented without options, leaving the people who are causing the problem with clear instructions to cease their behaviors or face specific consequences. In other cases, the parties will discuss and agree upon a solution.

Once again, leaders aren't doing this alone: they are guided by the seriousness of the problem, instructions from their superiors, and the legal liabilities and ramifications if the issue is not resolved. Each area offers unique guidance that, along with understanding the particular circumstances surrounding the problem, will help leaders identify the final resolution and the actions they need to take.

### Monitor the Solution

After a solution has been implemented, leaders should actively monitor the solution and periodically interview the employees affected to assure their satisfaction with the outcome. The leader's central purpose here is to ensure that the problem is completely resolved. If unresolved, then further action must be taken. Consequences may need to be revisited and more drastic action may be called for.

Leaders must understand that every complaint and problem is unique. Dealing with workplace issues means working with complex human behaviors that often have no simple or straightforward solutions. While some solutions are mandated by company policies or management direction, others require the leader's persistent application of logic until the problem is completely solved.

## POINTS TO PONDER — SOMETHING TO THINK ABOUT

1. How are you currently handling complaints? Have the results been satisfactory?
2. When facing a complex workplace issue, do you tend to avoid it and hope it goes away, or do you confront and handle it?

## TRAINING ACTIVITY — APPLICATION & ACTION PLAN

Create a decision tree to guide you in handling problems. Be sure to include each step discussed in this lesson.

1. Identify all of the possible options you have at each step.
2. Determine the actions you can take associated with each option (e.g. answer this question by filling in the relevant details: "If _____ happens, I need to _____).
3. Create a chart that details these options and possible choices.
4. Use it as a roadmap to a resolution when you receive a complaint.

# About the Author

Timothy F. Bednarz, Ph.D. is CEO of the American Management Development Group, Inc. For over 20 years he has researched, designed and authored hundreds of learning and development programs used by Fortune 1000 companies.

He is also the author of *Great! What Makes Leaders Great. What They Did, How They Did It and What You Can Learn from It* (2011).

## Speaking Availability

Timothy F. Bednarz, Ph.D. is available for speaking engagements for your next meeting or association event. He can be contacted at 800-654-4935 or by e-mail at timothy.bednarz@majorium.com.

## Bulk Sales

Bulk sales of this book or any other titles available from Majorium Business Press. Inquiries can be directed to sales@majorium.com, or by phone at 800-6654-4935.

# Quick Order Form

**Fax orders:** 715-342-1118. Send this form.

**Telephone orders:** Call 800-654-4935 toll-free. Have your credit card ready.

**Email orders:** sales@majorium.com

**Postal orders:** Majorium Business Press, 2025 Main Street, Stevens Point, WI 54481, USA.

**Please send the following books:**

________________________________________

________________________________________

________________________________________

________________________________________

**Please send more FREE information on:**

❑Catalog ❑Speaking/Seminars ❑Mailing Lists ❑Consulting

Name: ____________________________________

Address: __________________________________

City: ____________________ State: _____ Zip: _________

Telephone: ________________________________

Email address: ____________________________

**Sales tax:** Please add 5.5% for products shipped to Wisconsin addresses.

**Shipping by air:**

**United States:** $4.00 for first book and $2.00 for each additional product.

**International:** $9.00 for first book; $5.00 for each additional product (estimate).

Made in the USA
Monee, IL
04 November 2026

67377558R00031